IF ANY GODS LIVED
Copyright © 2018 By Michael J. Wilson
ISBN: 978-0-9991152-4-4
Library Of Congress Number: 2018964098

First paperback edition published by Stalking Horse Press, December 2018

All rights reserved. Except for brief passages quoted for review or academic purposes, no part of this book may be reproduced, stored in a retrieval system, or transmitted by any means without the written permission of the author and publisher. Published in the United States by Stalking Horse Press.

The characters and events in this book are fictitious or used fictitiously. Any similarity to real persons, living or dead, is coincidental and not intended by the author.

www.stalkinghorsepress.com

Design by James Reich
Cover Design by Max Neutra
Cover Photograph by Christian Michael Filardo

STALKING HORSE PRESS
Santa Fe, New Mexico

PRAISE FOR MICHAEL J. WILSON

"Wilson's debut, an amalgamation of biography, personal musing, and an obsession with electricity, constructs distinctive—and informative—narratives that revolve around the life of Serbian-American inventor Nikola Tesla. As he teases out facets of electrical history, Wilson broadens his focus to include Thomas Edison, Michael Faraday, and other inventors, as well as their inventions…Wilson gives shape and feeling to their lives, as when he writes in Tesla's voice, "I will build a city of light/ capture the sun/ drive my fists into the ground until I split the earth in two." This theme of light—and its iterations of lightning and electrical current—forms a brilliant and subtle thread linking many of the poems. Similarly, Wilson uses the past to tether his own story to something bigger."
—Publisher's Weekly

"*A Child of Storm* is charged with a seductive, sophisticated intelligence. Wilson's deft, deliberate, graceful poetics form a mesmerizing network of narrative and felt fragments that gain in power and resonance as the collection builds upon itself. The kinetic inventiveness of form and voice travelers a truly alluring structural path, and reward the reader with an addictive lyric hybrid of the historic and the intimate."
—Quintan Ana Wikswo, author of *A Long Curving Scar Where the Heart Shoud Be*

"To put it mildly, *A Child of Storm* is eloquently, elegantly devastating. If you want far reaching intellectual, economic and cultural injustice, the spiritual cost of human life, and grief that lands softly as pollen at dawn, this is the book to read."
—Genelle Chaconas, *Milkfist*

"Taken together, the effect is panoramic, taken individually, these poems are probing, lyrical, intimate. A series of history lessons, empathetic meditations on Tesla and on trees, love and 9/11, these poems crackle with energy and a compelling, intelligent calm that can ask unanswerable questions like, 'What does a glass of light look like?' and leave you sure that the truth is in the asking."
—Constance Squires, author of *Along the Watchtower*

"'The force that through the green fuse drives the flower / Drives my green age,' wrote Dylan Thomas, in lines that kept echoing through my head as I read Michael Wilson's striking debut. Anchored by poems about Nikola Tesla and poems about trees, *A Child of Storm* offers a stark and electric visual palette, as Wilson engages currents historical and personal, natural and made."
—Dana Levin, author of *Banana Palace*

ACKNOWLEDGMENTS

So so so many thank yous to my family, James Reich, Christian Michael Filardo, Max Neutra, D. Gilson, Dana Levin, Julia & Cameron Gay, Jon Quinn, and Sean Sunderland for all the ways they contributed to the building of these poems. Many thanks to the following for publishing pieces from this book in various forms:

Blood Tree Literature: "The Memory is Enormous" & "Ramble"
IDK: "Hard" & "Handkerchief Code : Black"
Indolent Books: "+"
Ping Pong: excerpts of "The Skeleton"

*

"Handkerchief Code : Red": quotes from a 30 October, 1990 House of Commons statement and 10 October, 1980 speech to the Conservative Party Conference by Margaret Thatcher

"+" quotes from "This Is This Dress, Aider" by Gertrude Stein

"Hostel Fuck": lyrics from John Cander and Fred Ebb "Cabaret" (1966)

"Handkerchief Code : Black": quotes from Frederick Buechner "Wishful Thinking" (1973)

"Handkerchief Code : Green": quotes a famously unverified John Wayne saying

"Handkerchief Code : Yellow": quotes from Ayn Rand "The Romantic Manifesto" (1969)

"Keith Haring": quotes from Keith Haring's personal journal

"Pepper LaBeija": quotes from the documentary "Paris is Burning" (1990)

"George Michael": quote from FKA Twigs "Glass & Patron" (2015)

"The Skeleton": quotes from Burt Bacharach and Hal David "I Say A Little Prayer" (1966) & the film "Mommie Dearest" (1981)

IF ANY GODS LIVED

MICHAEL J. WILSON

STALKING HORSE PRESS
SANTA FE, NEW MEXICO

CONTENTS...

I

+   13
Glory Hole   15
PnP   16
Parade   17
Attraction   18
Chute   19
Kiln   21
Handkerchief Code : Red   22
Sling   23
Hey   24
The Gay Bar   25
Glory Hole   26
Hard   27
Hostel Fuck   30
PrEP   31
Craigslist   32
Aubade   34
Handkerchief Code : Black   35
Ants   37
Three Ambiguities   38
Handkerchief Code : Green   39
Ramble   40
Unrequited   41
Gay Box   42
Handkerchief Code : Yellow   43

...CONTENTS

II

To the Sailor that Hart Crane Loved   47
Keith Haring   49
Sylvester   50
Auden's Circus   51
Frank O'Hara   52
Anthony Perkins   53
Pepper LaBeija   54
Rock Hudson   55
What's In Your Closet Dorian?   57
Robert Reed   58
Mapplethorpe   60
George Michael   61

III

The Distance Between What Is said + What Is Heard   65
Lass Meine Schmerzen Nicht Verloren Sein (for Mark Behr)   67
Quilt for April 2 2016   69
After   70
The Memory is Enormous   71
wolves – thirsting   74
I Am Clearly Still Angry   76
Pauses   77
Séance   79
Faggot   80

IV

The Skeleton   87

Hey faggot, better run learn to run cause Daddy's home
Daddy's sweet lil' boy, just a little too sweet
　　　—*Meshell Nedegeocello*

From this arises an argument: whether it is better to be loved than feared. I reply that one should like to be both one and the other; but since it is difficult to join them together, it is much safer to be feared than to be loved when one of the two must be lacking.
　　　—*Niccolo Machiavelli*

for Mark Behr,
you beautiful-terrible man

✚

You have AIDS

        have AIDS   what if

    you

          could be purified   in fire
set from the feather of a phoenix

               #beautiful#epic#blessed

   Aider,   why aider   why –

The ad on Craigslist has the face of a famous actor superimposed on the naked torso of Colby Keller
     the ad says 6'1"blk/bl175lb8.5thickuc   the ad says piss blood PnP 420 poppers must travel you host no fats no fems white only –

             Have + need –

   The ad says no bs   the ad says pic or no response

     whow   stop   touch –

    Hand under shirt – to the piercing – in my nipple

    There is that moment when the world seems
to spin out of control – when you could back out pant up + go – into the cold –

   the moment before fucking

     before too late to think about –

have AIDS have
      whow   stop touch,   aider   whow
                       All our sexual life we have been afraid
of getting having gotten had had having –

    because that is what happens

                      At the door to the building
take in the button you are about to press   imagine – the scent –

afterwards –

    on your fingers

GLORY HOLE

                    One of those apartment buildings –
name above the entrance –
            Lucille – Mary Belle –

    Brooklyn Heights – next door to a florist's
very upper middle

    The walk to the third floor is quiet – it's one of those places with one apartment on each floor one of those places that are quiet all the time – one of those places with bikes in the hallways

       There are options:

                    1)   the entry is hermetic sealed by a wood/metal/cardboard wall covered in black felt – there is just enough room to enter – stand – undress; or –
                      2)   a free-standing cardboard/particleboard wall – there's a room full of furniture/things/life – it is Lucy's psychiatry booth; or –
                      3)   Home Depot bathroom – a removable toilet paper dispenser – a rough-hewn hole – a scratching at the floor; or –

       He's probably on his knees – maybe a milk crate –

    If he's invested there's a TV playing maybe poppers maybe in the email before you specified str8 or gay + the screen is doing that thing you like –

                                          unzip –

place your cock on that expansive flat liver-colored tongue –

PnP

```
                                        + then
                    + −            then −

+ then + then
                 +
              look −        I'm not sure then + then look
       I'm not sure then look            don't − look then

+ then + then + then −
```

PARADE

       Cottonwoods
piss seed softness
      on us

Feel the glitter of asphalt in your knees – you
             are falling – you
     are running – you
             have jumped poorly the chain-link barricade –

             You just wanted some head – to give some head to
get some head – to have your dick out in the night

     to have some lips
             some tongue –

You notice blood on your fingers but can't check for wounds –

The seeds are blankets over the earth – they
                          should have cushioned
            there are so many –

You think about the time the bathtub overfilled
                      how you thought the world would fill

            how you still can't fathom why it didn't

ATTRACTION

I will make a list of things that make me feel good
will   , set it in amber   , or ice
leave it in my freezer so it is not used for frivolous things

I realize , the sound of snow
collecting in a field
I do not understand

my own taint
Easy   , be easy   , the sound
of snow , drifting the shed

Easy   , your finger   , paused
at the asshole   , tapping   , so lightly
                  , as if
you are doodling while on the phone

Cinnamon   , a sparrow color , hopping
along the worn edge of an empty fountain

I want to kiss you for hours

I am   , a being   , of tension

Easy   , be the sound   , of snow
on the precipice of avalanche

My list begins   + ends
with the same look

CHUTE

Fucking is unsafe – like
                        the view from the balcony

     You might imagine yourself into jumping

One hand on the rail
                so easy

     legs kick over then – almost
          flight

On the plane I imagine myself
knotted into ropes
tied – to the wings – the tail
the fuselage

                    I am a parachute

          opening skin behind the exhaust
     my atoms chemtrail the mid-west

Sex becomes a game

     rouletting cocks + balls in yawning mouths

I don't believe in bullets
just the death at the end of them

                In the dream of the sunken city

           a young boy imagines himself
     on dry land

      The moment before jumping – where
you could go back inside – close the door
drink water + ground yourself

liminal – a moonless night filling with mist

The fuzzy edge of the earth

Lightning across the dark expanse

It is a phantom phone call
                              a bulge
                              that is only a pleated shadow
                      deflating when pressed

      The wonders of windows
that don't open
                    or bars
bars are good

barriers galore –

                Don't tell me about the ways
            it could become safe

slides are always open on – at least – one end

KILN

Never more than one haphazard

humming static tear of flesh – a brush
of unfired glaze on white ceramic

The slip –

        Blood in a drain :
                sometimes honey
                sometimes the open mouths of calla lilies
                sometimes just pain –
                        an echo of the day – a smiling tooth-filled
face laughing on the TV –
      most of the time the blade dipped in ink scrawls over the
blank – image is clear as naked trees against a blue sky – a hovered
waiting –

Just a few words – never sentences

A quiet covers –

It's the tile – a soundproofing – the bathroom remains always a private space

Always bank to bank peaking in the hairline cracks
a press of finger into the center

                Never upstream never
                the open mouth of a vase

HANDKERCHIEF CODE : RED

      The man with the lines tattooed on his arm
takes his latte + moves across the room
with an easement that is enviable

the stench of appeasement

      in the air
      you have to be evasive

      the lines are sigils

      he stirs sugar packets into the hot drink
      inserts his finger
      tests the temperature

      how much
                  does
                           he take?

this lady is not for turning

            he's sizing the room – a redness there –
            thinking about who could take what

he runs fingers over the line near his wrist like a wedding ring

SLING

The whiteness of the house :
the beigeness of the house : the carpet
a rough-toed static :

The gold of the doorknob :
the greenness of the clicking lock : a momentary
blank in consciousness :

The sudden void : hologram of carbon : in the center of the room a
flat absorption :

an acrylic stool : a hole in the center :

    (image of a toilet of an ass of shit on a face)

The gunmetal of the rings : mounted to the wall :
the leather of the knotted cattail : sounding like snapping twigs : echo
of a dry cough :

    : legs above the head : above the heart :

        lube yourself :
        before he enters : bridle yourself :
        hitched : the sound of chain of birches in the wind :

HEY

There's a guy in Bed-Stuy with a big{9 inch}dick

                                            who will fuck you on his dinner table{large butcher block top{expensive]] while he watches [college]football on the TV in the corner{this isn't a metaphor for anything but it is A Thing]

                                                       He has blonde hair all over his body{that makes his body shimmer{like it's not entirely present{see:football]]
       he has a skateboard in the corner + he's 34 {the age you are now{not then{then you were 27]]]

   He'll be in your phone saved as 'Hey' {as in 'HAAAAAYYYYYY' as in '…you guys' as in 'YAS KWEEEN YASSSSSSSS' *finger snaps *head rolls *death drops but mostly as in 'you don't know his name + don't care']

                                       You will think about this guy for years{ten so far]
                                you will feel like a junkie{there will be no fix no rock pure enough the smoke will get in your eyes every time you see someone naked{+ every time you see someone blonde or someone who might skateboard + fuck while watching[college]football{this is not A Thing but is a thing]]]

THE GAY BAR

The bar is dark – a stick – my arms are trapped at my sides

I have never felt safe in queer spaces

When I was younger – I was so thin – so reedlike that I imagined myself on the banks of a marsh – a tower

leaning into the wind – alone on the bare rock – forever slipping – a space for electricity to strike + unstrike – but never ignite

At the bar I watch the glitter fall + it catches on my eyelashes

We are all beautiful + dirty

lost – we are avatars of ourselves

I order something – it comes out darkly – the room is a pulse of voices

Look – the fairies faggots deviants queers are out + I feel highlighted somehow other in the room of others

If I say
        I have never felt at home here – if it's true but sad that when I was younger I was desired by older men + then was not because I wasn't young enough or thin enough or hairless enough or –

        some other internalized shit

It is the sound of geese across the marshlands – an air horn in the hand of a drag queen – the noise as they catch fire

GLORY HOLE

Light begins to uncurtain – you can see it
        steady tide across a stone-covered yard

+ there – blooms unwrap themselves
        purple throats opening for light to pour into

HARD

Every time I put my dick in something I think about death

+ every time – I think of fingers raining like leaves

My aunt said *he's gay he's getting AIDS* –
$$\text{it was the tone}$$
$$\text{not the words}$$
$$\text{full of truth} –$$

The void of oppressive thoughts
     full of carnival music – an organ grinder
          a monkey in a little hat + vest on a unicycle refusing to stop –

I've always assumed that hell was Diana Vreeland's apartment –
contrasting patterns + the scent of peonies
causing the eyes to fuzz until you cannot discern color from self –

I would enter – thinking about death – + try not to place my nudity on her things

An eternity of trying not to place nudity
     anywhere –

When I was a boy the world had AIDS – it was on TV
        Magic + Freddie + Rock + that boy Elton John was friends with

In Africa everyone literally was dying of it – or of starvation

                                it's the same thing –

Peonies have developed the need for ants to crack their buds – the ants would starve without + the peonies would never bloom –

    this is a beautiful lie –

Every time I put my dick in something I think about death

The air is cold in this room – hums with the idea of being less so

It is Christmas + my aunt is dying – her head lolls between the TV selling jewelry + her lap – she is breast less belly button less nipple less –
                                          less less + less +
                                          less –

She tells me she loves me –

we sit in silence –

+ watch a giant amethyst spin slowly on a pile of ice

The little deaths – small like toys – the ones we can't hear – my death is one of those

This could be the time I start that death

Wind the turn-key on its back + set it off
        down the road with primordial clockwork scythe
                bubble solution Styx

I carry a coin I found on an airplane as it hovered in the liminal space

between day + night over the expanse of the dust bowl
                              – a yuan –

                                        the mandarin a series of
lines I will never transcribe – for the bubble boat man when it is time

Amethyst – a protector stone – preventer –
         its name comes from the Greek *a méthystos* –
                  to be not intoxicated
                           to never drink the poison of youth
                           to not find the waters of forgetting

                           when I put my dick in something –

HOSTEL FUCK

I'm not proud of barebacking across several continents

      but the water in the hostel was heated with solar panels so…

      You have to understand –

The smell of the shower stall :
    Clorox + overly perfumed body wash

I back onto his large Australian mushroom-headed cock –

      + the kids were fast asleep so…

      the way I am –

scalding water – like slapping ice

      mein herr

St. Theresa in East London

      walking barefoot across hot pavement an arrow through my heart

PrEP

      Those missile silos for sale in New Mexico + Kansas – what form would that spiral history take in your dreams –

      A wolf – like the one in Neverending Story – that nothing of clouds + fog + teeth – or the obvious bear wearing a fur cap with hammer + sickle –

      Wouldn't it probably just be a white guy in a three-piece suit always staring into the middle distance always smoking –

Say you buy one of these silos in Kansas or New Mexico – you start to stockpile water + canned food – for the end of time the apocalypse the zombie hoards –

      Can you smell the dampness – the circling empty space that haunts the center of the silo – is there a phantom rocket like a limb chopped + off thrown into a heap in a corner –

      + the water + cans in this underground castle – this prepping – what do these walls provide –

      The apocalypse has already occurred – the world was already destroyed – everyone got radiation got death –

      the cloud of our breath is a fog of war

CRAIGSLIST

There's this painting at The Met that was reframed to hide the top 8 inches —

forgotten – left in a closet – a century

    of keeping 8 inches hidden –

In the video they show holes from tacks driven through the canvas
    distant voices discuss how they will hide – will rehide –
    again fold over

the universe is a black hole – your eye enters the thought
    becomes trapped –
    lives 70,000 lives in a basement

I flip lotería cards like tarot
    at some point the universe hiccups – folds over it's upper third
  + pretends it never existed – the black hole
    has nothing to say

I pull the drunkard then the devil –

In the Craigslist ad you carefully fold parts into the background
    code hiding 8
        full
        inches

    for 100 years you will hide – will masc yourself –
tack marks protruding – you will wear out – need to be refurbished
– will find yourself staring at a video on the internet talking about you

as if you were an object in a museum –

You will want to rescue yourself

You will want to pull the tacks from the wood

You will hit reply – then send

AUBADE

A condom full of cum folds itself
on the floor like a finished lily – slick
with ass – the vanilla of latex fills the room

One drop moves towards the carpet – it is
sap season – March – melting floes
produce their sugars against the tidal waves of living

It is the smell that lingers in the aftersound of orgasm

Rain red light green lights its way down the window
that refracting – prism of stoplight outside
enforcing its realness into the room

A foot on the rubber – pedal down – etc.
sweat on the neck – drying flat of the river mouth

Who should sorry for stains – the murmuring
shadows of hair left on sheets that form a cloud
as cum cools separates –

swallows on oiled flesh

HANDKERCHIEF CODE : BLACK

Where does black fall on the spectrum?

        The question   is not about light
reaching from the recently eclipsed sun
        sliding   along sidewalks like water

        I'm asking because *God*   *occasionally*
drops   *a handkerchief*   a body   a season
an entire generation in the middle of the road like it's nothing

      I won't explain this to you
    this is not explainable
  go ask the Internet

 Years behind plywood doors   hearing music from the next room
muffled voices sex sounds amplified by giant speakers movie screens
a tap under the stall hiding hiding hiding from the gaze –

                I expect you to know this already –

    The chemical castration the re-education the therapy
electrocutions the religious belief in some high salvation –

        The dead from AIDS the dead from suicide the
dead from botched surgeries the dead from prison cells the dead
from the very light being cast out + forgotten by the sun –

           + if   the hankie dropped   is black

                some dominate submissive Old Testament
                    God must be a top thing –

        It would fall   leaves   or ash
touching no one it would land   drift into a gutter

                            bathe in the light of spring

These handkerchiefs are called saints
                      are burning   holes into our streets

ANTS

Ants like cum – the scent
as you crush them under your finger – sweet
candy – they have been infesting my apartment for years

I wake + the trail from the wall is a thread – a
wiry hair from below the carpet to the wall to the shelf
knitting the room – a seam beneath the boards

What the fuck do these ants want ?

With glasses on the trail is focused bodies – purposeful
it is moving to something – pink – fabric – a washcloth
cum rag

That phrase – diminishing – dehumanizing
orgasm – a broken spoke – distancing from lovelessness

Last night I pictured a former student + it didn't take me long

I console myself by remembering that he is 30

Ants – swarming – in over consuming the cloth

They couldn't care less about what I am thinking of

I peel the stuck object open – a sound of ripping proteins
like a seamstress ripping muslin – we are about to dressmake

Hundreds of bodies – picking monkeys grooming the fabric
the smell of their tearing – when I pour them in peppermint oil
the inevitability of death feels fresh – made new
like eyes after swimming

The room fills with green scent – the bodies grow still – the
thread a seam – an arm attached to the body – popping

THREE AMBIGUITIES

The dominatrix said she liked my tattoo
then complained
        about a missing pair of green leather pumps
        that might have cost $300 or $400
she licked a dog bone + passed it to her corgi

I dream about being suspended from meat hooks by dirty rope
knotted across my chest – the ribcage of a bird
around under my taint like mawashi
rubbing that velvet patch bare

The third shot of espresso leaves me
I move the ring
        from my left hand
        to my right middle finger
spin it aimlessly

Look at all these empty pairs of khakis

HANDKERCHIEF CODE : GREEN

Corners in the empty internet

        #hustle #fansonly

    In the discussion about sex work *a man has*
to have a code

        a list of things hanging by threads
        above the soon to ignite barrels of gasoline in the basement

        What does the ad say about
    the vanishing missing connections – hey

I was looking for _____

        but here is

      a tab on your tongue – *a creed* on your tongue

Notice the blinking out of places to find purchase

    the sound of elastic
        stretched across an ass cheek

    the sound of well-lubed fucking

Notice who gets to live and who
finds a fatal error

RAMBLE

Want

Maybe behind this
or that   sad bush

     there will be a future

          + then we could walk together awhile

       In the darkness of Central Park – lamps cast eggs of yellow
          safeties we could unmoor in

       If this bench were a blade –
your chest would render – would scatter into pixels –

The heart is a bubble

     wrapped in the petals of a moonflower attended by
hummingbird moths –

          We circle the lake that is not a lake

       We find the dark corners of a rock-filled hill – just want
       to be held – from the jaws of wolves

Each in our own way a sign of survival

UNREQUITED

Don't want	to look in	
your eyes	it ruins me	airlock
piñata	Christmas cracker	
all the small things		
will tumble	into space	

The butterfly net	has a hole	enough
for sparrows	to escape	
I am no Nabokov		
though	my obsessions	do pile

The canned air is a hiss		
something at the ear		
a memory of wanting		rush
hands	holding hands	

I picture myself alone in a field of stars
each eye a universe   slowly winding itself into itself
that we could be galaxies   colliding
+ not even know it

Your eyes are hard	to look at	are stars
+ each flit of sky a mote of dust		a sparrow
attempting flight in vacuum		

I want them	but I do not	want them
should not	want them	
they are wild	would remain so	

Movies have taught me the sound to expect when air is lost
At night I lie awake   the light
from outside   is unfocused orange

The face of it	open	unclosable
But never a sound		

GAY BOX

Dark like void – like behinds of eyes – not black – more like staring at the sun with eyes closed The walls are sticky – not tacky – more like the back of a stamp – sticker-y Smooth + never ending – on all sides a fun house mirror of something from childhood – obviously not childhood sudden realization of cocks A voice – a beat or the sound of death creeping up behind you whispering not to stop – keep moving – become buried in light

HANDKERCHIEF CODE : YELLOW

As a precondition of rebirth
                              we must wade

through the piss + shit + blood of that first birth

There were reports from the front lines that it felt like hell like limbo like a waiting room at a doctor's office   the reports talked about frozen feet limbs of black skin rolling like newsprint from the bone –

               Rebirth is not a Western concept +
                              every aspect of Western culture

      needs

Here is a box of handkerchiefs   they are brown + yellow + red I want you to mail them to the leaders of Western culture   want them to hang like rotting fruit from left or right pockets –

TO THE SAILOR THAT HART CRANE LOVED

I call the crane from its grave
                a kite of movement in + out of trees

          The unfinished bridge
          ink-cold waters – ill
   with the sickness of time – move greenly
beneath – despite this

Sailor – I bet you were beautiful –

We should not ask questions of the dead – but –

I want him to dance
with me – the way he danced with you –

Were you   worth the gilded armor
               the slipping into Troy under cover of night

     were you worth becoming myth for –

   + what did you do with the life he gave you
          wounded – flap of white in the periphery

     the crane would know surrender as well –

Did you go to the unfinished bridge – the cracked
          missing span – your toes
          on the edge

                did you toy with leaping off – not
                that you should have – not
                that you deserved to –

A wound   delirious – in the center of my head
                 this not my pain – look

the horizon is a mass of wings – did you
like the attention – did he
kiss you too hard – feathers falling over you like snow –

was he a stone in your hand.

KEITH HARING

    If revelation –
    If sphere of head –
    If bendy arms –

    The lines of my face are bold – they heart
dance
            heart dance

                          The fear – *in fact*
              the symptoms already –

                                A balloon –
       strikes   the groove – *watch*

this kind of slow death –

I am abducted by flat aliens in the gallery

    everything is like humidity.

SYLVESTER

      Those days in the caftan – ones
           unreal broken
         – look glitter
                  always

              look smiling – sweat
must be from dancing – always

By 15 I knew how to mask – lace
the beak-nose swirling thing over

my eyes darkening – the scent of roses – look
like ring lights – kiki over coffee – no plague here
                                           – always

I place the crumpled roses in my pocket – unreal
the safety – look sidewalk – asphalt – knees

When we go out we carry our history – we
look sweat – glisten lip – lace at the neck

Mighty sequin over the eye – a coin clasping – always
for the ferryman – on Bleaker on Christopher

speaking in tongues – the panic of it – here
is my face – doubling – you get this side today – for
      real – only this side.

AUDEN'S CIRCUS

We considered the basements of Disney World
in the classroom with Auden a circus came about us
the folds of canvas an armor – the sound of
mourning doves a wooden spool downhill –

I came home + turned all my shit upside down
looking for the ways things hide themselves
I don't see the clown in time –
                                    Is there a time clown? It
finds told-you-so's in life + dissects them in death –

Press ice to the forehead + discover that to
damn it all up + down we must
find the moment that the basement started itself – must
become that pitied cellar full of costumed heroes

The seams of the chair are the lines between thighs –
that worries me. Everything is a potential problem
surfacing like whales from the depths of the basement of the world
to die on beaches
                    to be mistaken for folklore.

FRANK O'HARA

New York is the vertebrae of a young man's spine
+ you are a walking
avatar in a suit + tie

Your newspaper is prominent

This is not Whitman in the grocery store
you don't shop like that

you find apples on the street
rolling in the gutter you polish them til they produce a clear staccato

Gardenias in the ductwork
frames upon frames
artworks hinge toward your pressed starched tie

Men stiffly bend their suits toward you

You wake with the sun then you sleep with it.

ANTHONY PERKINS

The spider crawls from the wig –
            the attic –
                      the closet – I mean – a thread of tragedies
                      a finger pointing towards the cliff face
                      saying – there – tragedy

      An airplane attacks a building – 41.5 million people will be lost

The tragedy is that you are silly – that you flop around
that you are debased rebased – are set on your way –

            but the way is a loop
        the house is always the same – the grin an opening void
   if the moment unhinged –

Spooky underdone trope of the over-mothered
                Do – not – be – one – of – THOSE – boys

My limp wrist – the noodliest appendage loping tentacle at your
Adam's apple

Cue sounds – ch ch ch ch ah ah ah ah –
        the crack of the shell that is your neck –
                ketchup pouring down the drain.

PEPPER LABEIJA

                The printer
          is running out of ink

+ we are only at the nipple

Dial-up was a pain – the sound of it
still a trigger of gay panic

                    Imagine the secret folder
              worn about the edges
                         blue boy – full of home
                         printed porn

    When you're gay
    you monitor everything you do

      The words in the chatroom – the sound
              of that ding – that they responded – that
                        they also want dick

Your mother will find it – the blue folder
will throw it into the street light it on fire – she
              will know too much

This ain't no girl's coat – this is your coat

                  Fucking on the floor
        of a gas station
                at 16

      Feel alive in that moment – be the fire
give yourself some
walking room.

ROCK HUDSON

Gotta get that baritone masc
that look – the eye – that climbed-a-mountain chin
if not – might as well kill yourself –

First –

      – not first but – first
      a dynasty a day a giant
         – that first

Tab Hunter underbussed – Nabors Pyled – Rory Calhoun cancered
that wake –
    a ship in a bathtub
    catching in a drain – to have the balls
        to burn it all down behind you –

Heart attack bloom –
Television bloom –
A skipping memory –

On the screen in 84 –
    a wreck of pillows – becoming the first first
        the most first
        so ahead the denials felt fresh

In the dusty rose covered sun draped moments – fingers
worrying the threadcount of the brocade are a concern

    Golly Rock –
    I can see you

A pile of pills feels like a trending topic

Who will be our Doris Day – the reflection can
hardly bother a flat iron press bleach curl – how can it

        crawl from the mirror – pluck the bottle
            press hair into place on our head

                find a soft lit Vaseline lens so we can go on.

WHAT'S IN YOUR CLOSET DORIAN?

      I want to take the orange candy corn + melt it down – rub it into my shadows until the blue is covered

I watch from the depths of the closet – I'm a closet monster –

                          [what are you seeing? is it lovely + flawless? does it have claws covered in green nail polish? is it named dion? is it hairless + barely legal? would you fuck it?]

Dorian who is this corpse I'm hungry –
        covering it in tulle won't un anything – the pasties cover your eyes they tassel in their sockets – I'm still rubbing the candy into my face trying to un-male myself –

      what is your excuse for the mounting darkness
                    for the piles of gender under foot.

ROBERT REED

        See   ,   there   ,
        the suburban sprawl   ,   of your hair   ,

That staircase   ,
        I wanted it   ,

wanted my fingers to
      tie   ,   untie ,
           knot over everything

But that staircase went nowhere – TV lies TV
smoke
            reflected monsters –

Let the turtleneck eat you – wrap
your neck until you are silent

Let the staircase descend –

      You   ,   + Darth Vader
      are my father

      The room
will allow you to be the man you always wanted

You can get your car in the garage

      Now ,
         unclock ,
      here   ,

A bridegroom – a fence a body
filling tangle of astroturfed white space

The absence –

Not
        a void   , though   ,

                      imagine all of America
                      fatherless   ,

        riding bikes
        in circles at the end of a cul de sac.

MAPPLETHORPE

Let's talk about
the
                                 sword knife-pressed
       on your rectum –

                break it at the hilt

In the beginning there was fucking
       the concept
       the wanting

+ then there was the reality of it
of leaving oneself inside another

That night we sat across from each other +
we stared into the table +
our eyes could not find focus –

        + I want to fold myself
                into a ball   cut off
      my genitals
      place them in a jar of vinegar
      leave them under bridges as a tithe for crossing
      + that is such bullshit

Our skin shines in the light
gilds – marbles – enters the realm of permanence

Our mouths –
           a drama that repeats daily.

GEORGE MICHAEL

The denim hips – white
tee pulling at the hairless edge of skin

      Freedom + exploding closets –

           what sort of earthquake – the breaking juke box

                I realized sex in a bathtub
                as far from Cindy Crawford as one could be

+ that drip in the background –
                in water blood turns into bug-eyed goldfish
        I am a Pisces that cannot
manage both directions – cannot boom or bust chains

but can manage the drain – I

      want to imagine your face + I see
      a shadow of beard resting Dali clock over the sink

The mask – a nightgown darling –
on a chair by a moonlight –
            a claw-footed field –
                a chair of brambles digging into the arm –
fuck me while I stare at the sun

Roses
      down the arm – a crown of sonnets –
      your feet soaked in MDMA.

THE DISTANCE BETWEEN WHAT IS SAID + WHAT IS HEARD

My grandmother asks from the backseat : *Why don't you have a girlfriend?* –

   ---crickets---
        have as much protein as two eggs they

taste like a field of hay
    drying at the end of the season

      the breeze comes – your mother's hand
across your hair when you have a fever on

Hallowe'en – knocks at the door – small
hands holding pillow cases
        plastic pumpkin buckets – small mouths wanting
     the broken line of desire to be filled
  with anything

They taste like a conversation
     spoken in single word tweets
          delivered – one a day
over the course of years –
          you've missed a few
the meaning is discernable – the holes are deep –

She's in the back seat + the car is inches from swerving into traffic
jumping the median – the line of barriers – flipping in the air – a gymnast
    not falling
       but not winning gold –

  it would freeze there

         Yeats' falcon

        loosed from the

                dying landscape – sudden repeating wings – multiple heads – a seraph of spinning wind in a door –

    tires a cacophony of spinning grip

I would tell her about the man I let fuck me on the banks of the Gowanus at 2 in the afternoon – show her the doctors bills from the third time I had gonorrhea

        would become a thousand-winged voice – the legs of crickets in media res

Kill the already dead

What answer can silence the silence

LASS MEINE SCHMERZEN NICHT VERLOREN SEIN

Look – ! – at all the dead queer bodies

Hate crimes tick in the background
        There are dreams about diffusion
        about accounting for the number of deaths :

    1 2 3 4 5 6 7 8 9 1million

A nest of wires is both bed + coffin
Lashing you to a fencepost in Wyoming

A scissor that will only cut once –
        it is cold is itching
        the sound of a car refusing gear

All these queer bodies being laid to rest
will not rest how could there be rest rest is not coming

I woke up early to write this – I began to write this

I learned of your death –

                fuck you –

            I begin again

      I covet the ability to be happy about being able to walk
down the street without being murdered –

    – desire to be normal safe unthreatening normal not broken sane
normal not sad or dying or deviant but always deviant + never normal –

we live in a time where neuroses masquerade as progress –

I just want to hold your hand I just want to hold
your hand I just want to hold your hand I just want to
not fuck tonight + to hold your hand

       To take the masc from my face – untie the silken ribbon across
the back of my head feel that waterdry smoothness let go of my skin –

Wouldn't that be lovely + beautiful

It's complicated – I'm complicated – who isn't complicated

At the party that wasn't about you but might as well have been
someone said
our greatest accomplishment was to be seen straight

The laughter was nervous sharp then silent

Too much treble too much volume

       unequalized values in the room armored an echo
       switched the kill gauge to 1 2 3 4 5 6 7 8 9 1million

There was silence +
     queerness
     a pink highlighter across a clean white book

The molecules of it coalesced + spun violently in the center of the room

QUILT FOR APRIL 2 2016

On the last day of March it begins to snow + it continues into April + that line about black boughs + cruelty echoes across the New Mexico landscape like a dirt devil full of tumbleweeds

I ask the woman behind the counter what I want there's a silence between us that would be hilarious if it wasn't insane

The pictures of the quilt across the National Mall – the largest bed in the universe – rest your head on Lincoln's lap + stare into the dome of the sky + what sort of dream is there in that circular night – is it a mirror of the day that happened or one of the future

Wrap the cloth around you + roll in the grass until everything is covered in green until your skin is stained with life

The week old baby is asleep + I can't help but wish that the future will be better his parents are there + we all kind of nod in agreement – it's dark + sad + maybe inappropriate but it's the truest thing that has ever happened in the world

AFTER

There are times
I think about your eyes

The rest of you
disintegrating – dead pixels on a television

A sticker rubbed until white

Ink – peeling diseased toenails
layers of birch bark rolling to the waiting ground

The memory leathers

THE MEMORY IS ENORMOUS

.

I sit in the dark of the room
The lights from a police car turn
red   then blue   then

      the books on the shelves seem hesitant

.

If I say that I loved you - that it really fucks me up to think about it
+ that ends a season before it begins –

Will someone please turn off the alarms

      In the street
      there is a car
      + it has run into something
      + that something is an echo

.

There is that drive to the airport

An image of all the wrong – spinning in some pocket of time
like a goddamn metaphor for everything – there it is

life caught by the grill of an SUV on the highway
murdered like some cow –

I raise the blackjack + think about what body to place under it

.

The dark is carbon paper

+ the trapped object is a dog – wild or otherwise

the body of which – is cartwheeling

.

Here is what happened:

    The dog ran across three lanes of highway
    Barely making it – I almost was the one –

    + I caught my breath
    as it reached the median
    + I prayed as if I believed in God that it would stop + sit + be still –

    It made it two more lanes – this dog – running like something was chasing it

    The grill of the SUV
    Silver – breaking light like water

        + the dog's body was unhinged
                It tore a hole in space

It spun like a top – like some stuck
                perpetually spinning thing

    I know because I began to scream + –

the cars slowed down to look – to see

a newly formed black hole

.

+ what I'm not talking about is that I was picking you up at the airport

    that this is so difficult

that it was some kind of warning
that it was the last time

I was driving towards you + the lights were flashing
red   then blue   then

+ instead of stopping I kept screaming + crying + screaming + I was driving + then I saw you + your eyes + then the moment + the moment in duplicate + then the moment repeating until the end of the universe + –

.

I was waiting in the dark for the lights to stop so I could go to sleep

So time would stop holding its breath

WOLVES – THIRSTING

The whole time we were together
I dreamt of home invasions

In my head – I am hard-
wired

        It's not love – that
        is some warm pancake shit

A thing on TV – what I am saying is

        that fucking is not love –

the second you're holding hands
someone will throw a bottle at your head
chain you
        to a fence
                beat you to pulp

            leave you to die

So when we were together –

I had a hard
time of it – I couldn't see into
the face of it – was shadow – was
the river I'd drown in

They'd come in the night –

I never slept

the entirety of our relationship – never

                          one full night

They'd come + find us faggots in bed
they'd kill you – take
you from me – leave
me alone – the dreams – faces
at the windows – wolves – thirsting

I AM CLEARLY STILL ANGRY

The clay pots sit where they were left in the fall – waiting – filled to the brim with last year's soil – the small rocks lining the bottoms of them taken from that house with the rose bush I endlessly obsessed over – caring more about its limbs than my own –

The sound of their breaking – imagine the sound of fired clay against concrete – the breath being pushed from the lungs of a body being beaten to death – ribcage cracking like kindling on a fire the wood so wet that all it produces is the smell of furnaces –

I want to promise that they will be protected from this – that they will have seeds in them – will have new sprouting heads – that I will not throw them one after another towards the highway that spirals into the distance like a great rubber band across the landscape –

But I can't keep secrets – + I hate the idea of things growing from these shells + I want them to sit dumbly in the rain the wind the blistering heat of summer – I would only plant to watch the green shoots turn yellow + white + wither –

I am clearly still angry –

But let this emotion enter + absorb the room – here the pots become vessels for something greater than growing – they are where we can place our organs as our bodies empty – I feel the pain in my back becoming greater – let me put my kidney here just for a moment –

The heart fits nicely in the small urn that had alyssum in it – purple flowers pop across the surface like barnacles – that we had that kind of water – that those small beak mouths could open + find their peace – that the sun wouldn't need so much from us –

How does the soil know when it is time to squeeze the roots until they break – that winter is coming – that the trail of vines is also a lower intestine – fuck these branches needing to be pruned – + these fingers for tracing the buds like life signs no one will notice the fresh scent of green anyway –

PAUSES

In chrome
tooth – carved – human
a mat of hair

dipped in the blue
of your eye – look – ! – ocean

shells of dead things

...

The lake is a sieve
a marrow – I am
waiting for Jason Voorhees
to kill me –

In the cold of this
a greening – your eye again – the lake
tiny universe –

If it be it be good
somewhere in memory
an oak leaf – gilt-charred
about the edges

...

The box is taped
but this hardly describes
that it has been taped
full of monsters – it

is your teddy bear –

...

I write about us too much
our honestly short run
but I unbox us again

+ again

like some gaudy holiday decorations

I should make a video
me – unboxing
a sinking ship

I am listing

Are you listing?

That's the real trouble

...

I tape the box shut
it screams

I imagine you able to ignore it

SÉANCE

If any gods lived we knew them not

The candles will not light they collapse

In thaw the river is a damless removal

Worm casings

Sounds of grunting

The earth is a resonance machine

Hands across the table across the expanse between buildings

We pour ourselves from ruin to White House lawn

The magnolia tree blooms are an injury

A bandage stuck in hair

FAGGOT

I hide

        the word   after

                I type it

      I don't want to upset
      the thin veil of the coffee shop

An embarrassment – I look around – see pink everywhere

The dead are not looking –

I think about your body
                      the angles
         of it – I know
this will embarrass you – so
                          I think about it more

                Right now

I am thinking about your fingers – the blurry tattoo
    LUST
               in the pit of your forearm

Your body is every body I have been with
this is unfair to everyone in the world

                Every single fucking time –
                    I type it

      erase the thought of it

      become angry at the thought of it

      place the thought of it on a pile of sticks + light it

Think about the times I've been tossed – the sound
someone yelling faggot across the abyss – a snarled
child-dog on a leash

            Then I am angry at the comparison – but
                I still imagine slapping the child

Think about reclamation – taking
owning + then wearing it on a t-shirt

Broken plinth to the martyred homosexual

Atop two men fuck – coated in glitter – staring
at every eye staring back at them

I don't want to write about victims

I don't know how to not be angry with myself

I think about your body – the smell
            of cigarettes +
roses –
      a sign of the dead
                trying to communicate
                with the living

The eye of the wasted man met mine on the street corner
                  desire – because I want
        to tilt the room – I stare back –

I realize that I think about things until I care about them

I joke that we should turn the land over + sow it with salt
The joke becomes less funny – then
                a viable alternative – then
                a reality

The safe gay – the one the men can fuck
while highdrunkgone – can
                            write away as
      a
                  one
                          time
                                  thing

On new years he asks about gay sex

        How.

        It.

        Works.

Salt the earth – think about
bodies in a void of white – think
                              about a finger –

        I fall for this every time –

later I let him inside me because he's surprisingly good at giving head

    The sound of confetti

Are you drunk enough to admit you want it
to feel the thing – I am

                always

                            so fucking sober

I want to remember the darkness in my own eyes
        I type that – look into it – erase it

I put on amethyst-colored underwear
        to feel safe – to line myself

        I accidently type "lie" – erase it
        start over

Under the lights of the gas station I scream until I taste bile

The snow looks like glitter

I think about your body – fingers – a floating
        device that is a collar bone – I think
    I could call
    this anger – sadness – anger – lust

If the heart is a well – a fist – a broken wave
        the mind is a moon pulling tides

I stare into the darkness – there is reflection

I type – hate myself – erase it

I type – angry with myself – erase it

I type – sound of loud music thrashing in the back alley – flash of glitter – the moon at full in a parking lot in Brooklyn – the crack of your body as it turns into a key + opens into an expanse growing enveloping a wave a scent an impact –

I think about my body against yours

I want these things to be pure from our histories

I want to save them from the fire

I type – erase –

    the word + then

        I erase it

IV

THE SKELETON

.

At the base of the herniated disc
an ooze pulse of pain

I knot my fingers
into that tail space + my skin makes room

like that time in the Temple of Doom
fingertips   push   in – easy – so easy

I become a mass
of hot tar on the road

flesh on the spine – a humpback
breaching for air

+ when it exposes itself
the unified panel of a frame of film skids then bubbles

in the sharpness of sudden air

Here into my hand the green of spinal fluid – endless

pouring of biohazards powdered marrow – my spine sucks
from my body – pools on the floor – leaves me

I kick against the birth – it brings
all it can carry from within + slinks into the corner to sleep

Red poinsettias on a red plane
the table set for Christmas – for 15
a cabinet – of glass – a fire – of glass :

>   Your grandmother would take
>   the bones into her mouth – suckling crack
>   of them then tongue of them :

    All is dead then buried then explored as a beautifully abandoned place
        whose hand is this clasping this ring – an infinity of abandonment
        the spider-like fingers a webless state :

I cannot bear to see these histories like this – find the idols
the broken statues of ancestry – tie these bones
to those bones

.

      I want – my thumb
the bone
              polished – left
on the shelf with the chocolate chip cookies

      I want my joints in your packed lunch
behind peanut butter + jelly

wrapped in plastic – oils – your fingers
            all over – I
                    don't know how
                    to say I love myself

            but – I – don't
    know
how to say I hate myself

I don't want to die –

I want to be liquid – pool across the room
      be ooze –

           taste
           this

           O god –
take my knuckle in your mouth
      roll it across your tongue
            let me rubber + disintegrate –

Since I am boneless
in a grocery store –

The Skeleton wants to push the cart + –
there is no argument –

    I fit myself in to a jar that fits in the child seat

The Skeleton wants to buy moisturizers :

The Skeleton wants to buy bleach :

    recent skinlessness is the color
    of adobe baking in the sun

We trace aisles – buy air fresheners in tropic themes
    a gallon of mayonnaise
    the day-old ends of bread

    a can of spray-on snow

We pay with a toe bone + a rib

.

I push –

                                       the swing

       goes   forward

       up

I am left in that gravity-less space
watching chains

                       seat

                               passenger

     expand

     in the air

You feel the pull of it ?

Like you were going to drag behind – like
some rednecks tied you to a truck –

I draw three coins

                 clarity

                       peace

    dissolution

I hum a mantra + stare at the nude space

     waiting

for the swing – the body
to come back

like a camera on auto-focus – the sun a ring

a ring

a bell in a church
       a burned memory

Here comes the swing

     carrying bones

I Force = Mass x Acceleration –

My palms white from pressing –

The Skeleton raises thin interlocking radii + ulae

     mouth open
          teeth shining

   The Skeleton
   kicks its femurs

         jumps –

     .

                     You sit across from me

        holding out a single
        yellowed finger

in a pleading Oscar Wilde way

        dirty
                 dressed
in blood still

Tendons connect us –

long graypink things across the chasm
of the living room

living room

                living   room

I kneel   am praying   the

dusty brown curtains thin to stained glass

Lighting the old orange candle that smells like candy
I look into eye sockets as if you are a priest

My eyes cataract spider + pop   they
      crystalize
             under pressure
             I become glass I fill I rupture

The Skeleton
    sits at the mirror humming

           I say a little prayer for you
    It puts on make up

Delicate pinked brush over slicing cheekbones
         the powder sticking to no pores

The room is bathed in candle light is papered in purple is
        wrapped in roses

     the whispersound of a fan

Like Joan Crawford –

    His endless dark socket eyes
         Don't fuck with me fellas

  He stands
  sprays his ribcage with perfume

Eye shadow purple as a bruise
      The Skeleton turns
       spreading itself   flayed ribcage

     stares into the doorway
    where I watch

Then
it asks about dead relatives
asks me to lie back
put my head in the basin
allow it –

    to wash my hair –

There is tapping on the window

    like impatience – like a blind cane

like the wind – like an unshut gate

Tell us about your day dear Tell us about your boyfriendgirlfriend dear Tell us about what you do for a living or where you live Tell us anything really What do you think about the weather or the telly or that whatsherface who stole soandso's man…

One twig finger

    along the line of an ear

Since I am boneless :
    I disrobe
    stare at the skin before me
    think about the thinness of the architecture

At night The Skeleton sits
              cross-legged
    on my chest
        like a cat

At the slightest noise :
    flick of neck
    radar dish of danger
    twitch at the jawline

Without structure skin cannot –

    I imagine myself old
              then dead
       then dust

The Skeleton thinks about nothing
    stares into my pigeon chest
    at the remains of my chest
    opens me like a chest

The sun – blinding – baking

The Skeleton holds a hand to its forehead

It bends
       extending
       one arm down +
       grabs the knob of bone at the ankle

  from the heel – or some secret place
  The Skeleton pulls

thick
gray
rope of tendon – stretches – extends

       +
       looking at me – dark void eyes dark
       void teeth –

The Skeleton
a lover offering his hand
a silence between the offering + the offered –

  Its eyes –
  that darkness where there should be eyes

I take the tendon – my tendon –

       wrap
       the cold cord around my arm +
       drag the thing through the yard

You walk along the edge of the world
which is the edge of the roof of a childhood home

The roof slick with night   is dangerous

Arms stretch out
                       present figurehead
                       a seagull
          a cross

You cannot speak – mime the lyrics to some pop song

One hinged foot in front of the other
pressing down the calcaneus – tracing a

back + forth motion from breast bone to nothing

hands back + forth back +

     Like that –
                I think

I hold your hand
+ we watch the sun rise

The horizon turns purple then pink then white hot

I feel my heart beating + hold
branching fingers to my chest –

Spineless – a cackle
from the hollow tree

The jelly of us – we are liquids afterall

I place my hand
on the back of my spine

The tail piece – final resisting bump

That painful vertebrae

Press fingers there – pull – realize I have done this before

Pool in the brain – reeds
catching fire by the marsh

The marsh catching dryness

I lay the bones – like alms – proverbs
in a brass bowl

Piles of calcium
you will ignite now
golem self

I rub the mud at the joints
scribble words on paper – place
under the jawbone

Grapple with the remaining marrow on my fingers
make a broth – feed it to the cat – to myself

ABOUT THE AUTHOR

Michael J. Wilson lives in Santa Fe, New Mexico where he writes for an arts and entertainment company. *If Any Gods Lived* is his second book of poetry.

wilsonmj.com

ALSO BY MICHAEL J. WILSON

A Child of Storm

www.ingramcontent.com/pod-product-compliance
Lightning Source LLC
Chambersburg PA
CBHW030454010526
44118CB00011B/937